MW00778152

CHANEL

Fine Jewelry

First published in the United States of America in 2000
by UNIVERSE PUBLISHING
A Division of Rizzoli International Publications, Inc.
300 Park Avenue South
New York, NY 10010

and

THE VENDOME PRESS

Copyright © 2000 by Éditions Assouline, Paris
Translated from the French by Chanterelle Translations, London

Front cover photograph: Diadem *Franges* in platinum and diamonds, created by Chanel for
her collection of haute jewelry in 1932. Photo: © Robert Bresson/Chanel Archives
Back cover photograph: Adrienne necklace and Cocarde earrings in 18-carat yellow gold,
cultured pearls, and diamonds. Photo: © Tizano Magni

ISBN: 0-7893-0468-6

Color Separation: Gravor (Switzerland)
Printed and bound in France

Library of Congress Catalog Card Number: TK

2000 2001 2002 2003 / 10 9 8 7 6 5 4 3 2 1

CHANEL

Fine Jewelry

By François Baudot

UNIVERSE / VENDOME

to M.L. C.T.

By good fortune, she has retained nothing in herself,
of the contagious brilliance of gold,
that indiscreet light exuded by weak beings overburdened with property.
COLETTE, Prisons and Paradise, 1932

P ioneer of twentieth-century fashion, and the first dress designer ever to have successfully launched her own range of perfumes, Gabrielle Chanel was one of the most famous women of her time. She is less well-known as a designer of platinum and diamond jewelry, however, and it is her fascinating foray into the world of jewels which is traced in this book. The current direction taken by the house of Chanel, in the spirit of its founder, includes the creation of high-quality jewelry just as she designed it half a century ago, when her motto was: "I want to be part of what is going to happen."

"If I chose the diamond, it is because it represents the highest value in the most compressed form. I used my love of everything which glitters in an attempt to combine finery, elegance, and fashion." In 1932, Chanel made this peremptory statement to deny one of her claims to fame, namely elegant dressing on a budget and its corollary, costume jewelry. She was the first of the great Parisian couturiers to use artificial jewels and she used them to great effect from the outset, since they featured prominently in her fashion shows. Indeed to such an extent that she declared, a feminist in spite of herself, "A woman's décolletage is not a strong-room!"

In the earliest years of the century, long before the impoverished, enigmatic, highly ambitious young girl called Gabrielle Chanel had begun her career, first as a milliner, then as a dressmaker, yellowing photographs demonstrate her disdain for all the outward trappings of wealth. As someone who was locked in secret battle with an entire sector of society, those whom fortune had favored and who would never have allowed a woman in her station of life to rise to greater things, she rejected outright the dress conventions of turn-of-the-century France. It was through this rejection, criticism, and manifest disgust that the marginalized Chanel would amaze, seduce, and finally proclaim her difference. With her sporty jersey fabrics, little black dresses, figure-hugging clothes, slim lines, bobbed hair, and sun-tanned skin, the couturière transformed her contemporaries with her revolutionary look, coinciding with another revolution taking place in the arts, architecture, and poetry. The Roaring Twenties, which the French call the "Mad Years," were also the years of Chanel's greatness. As a latter-day Goddess of Reason, her message would be heard and ideas embraced instantly, joyfully, and without a backward glance, as fashions are wont to be.

mademoiselle Chanel's exhibition of fine jewelry, held from November 1 to 15, 1932, in her townhouse at 29, Faubourg-Saint-Honoré, Paris, caused a sensation. The exhibition, designed by the famous couturière, displayed a collection of the most magnificent diamonds. Coco, as Parisian society had already dubbed her, was at the height of her success. Furthermore, with her $N° 5$ perfume, she had managed to invade the jealously guarded prerogative of the perfumers, demonstrating that a great dress designer could launch a perfume. All that remained for her was to conquer the domain of real jewelry, another sacrosanct preserve, in which the "Grande Mademoiselle," the queen of costume jewelry, still felt she needed to prove herself.

"Chanel is the only Auvergne volcano which is still active." This is how her contemporaries described this orphan who had decided to conquer the age in which she lived. Fine jewelry, like perfume, was an essential part of the high life that Gabrielle adored. Luxury was reassuring. Later, it helped to fill a loneliness as big as the Ritz Hotel. Furthermore, jewelry was the perfect counterpoint to her androgynous figure. Her detractors said she had the body of "an undernourished little telegraph girl." They were forgetting that post office employees were unlikely to have grand dukes, millionaires, and poets at their feet, great men who were often remarkable and always ready to weep rivers of diamonds. Each of the jewels that Mademoiselle Chanel owned— and her jewel-case was one of the most opulent of the century— brought her the certainty of having been loved by men who had paid a high price for her favors. It was also the certainty, because gemstones cannot lie, of having had the last word. And that was something Mademoiselle really valued, far more than the gems that she had always combined indifferently with coloured paste and junk jewelry. It added to the confusion when she secretly had copied for her own personal adornment—but using genuine precious stones this time— some of the costume jewelry sold by her fashion house. "It's fake," she would explain with disarming sincerity of her own finery of Byzantine or Coptic inspiration, and the stones were indeed so large that few doubted they were artificial.

Rubies, emeralds, sapphires, topazes . . . of all her jewelry, Mademoiselle Chanel preferred the magnificent oriental pearls which she wore on any occasion, including, to the stupefaction of the gentry, when she went riding with her lover, the Duke of Westminster. Pearls with tweed! Nothing like it had ever been seen before. But had a former *grisette* ever been seen prancing like a roe deer alongside the most powerful man in England? For her clients, the couturière would do something similar, pouring cascades of overtly fake imitation pearls over black jersey. Here again, it was as if it were all a game, a guessing game to distinguish the real from the false, a game of deceptive appearances, anticonformity and antisnobbery. There was nothing in this that would give the jewelers of the Place Vendôme anything to worry about. At least, not yet.

A party of grave-faced gentlemen, made even more grave-faced by the Depression, began turning up at Mademoiselle Chanel's headquarters in the early 1930s. They represented the Union of Diamond Merchants. These were the people who controlled the most valuable deposits of gemstones in the world, who governed the price of the stones, ensured that they retained their mythical aura and guaranteed their brilliance and prestige. The terrible slump that had hit Europe had forced them to take drastic action. In this case, they decided to knock on the door of one of the most famous and creative women of the day—who happened to be the very person who had witheringly scorned the security and value of expensive jewelry. Chanel kept her cool. She listened to their arguments, and an appetite for diamonds as a symbol of authenticity, clarity, and brilliance began to grow in her changeable mind. She would be the leader of the pack, fighting for the best, the most expensive, the rarest. She requested, and was granted, *carte blanche* to go into action.

t he result of this meeting between the Grande Mademoiselle and the gentlemen of the diamond industry soon became apparent. In 1932, the first day of November dawned with grey skies. Chanel had chosen All Saints' Day to issue one of her rare invitations to a few select members of the elite who were still known as *Le Tout-Paris*. At the time, she was living—renting, of course, she never owned her own home—two floors of one of the most magnificent mansions built for French aristocrats in the eighteenth century. The Hôtel Pillet-Will was next to the Elysée Palace (formerly the Hôtel d'Évreux). It had a courtyard and the garden spanned the Faubourg-Saint-Honoré and the Champs-Élysées. The suite of rooms on the ground floor were clad in period white-and-gold painted wood paneling and mercury-backed mirrors. Chanel changed nothing, only adding a few of her favorite creature comforts, a few deeply upholstered sofas, satin-covered couches, and an antique marble statue as a symbol of timeless, classical Greek beauty, a masterpiece that she kept with her throughout her life. The bronze fire-dogs in the neoclassical fireplaces had been sculpted by Jacques Lipchitz. A pair of these magnificent abstract bronzes can still be seen in the apartment occupied by Chanel until the end of her life (now reverently preserved at 31, rue Cambon). Completing the personal touch in the form of accessories were the famous black-and-gold Coromandel lacquer screens which she made fashionable; their panels unfolded in mute, oriental luxury, creating a few intimate corners in the grand style architecture that surrounded then.

"Through the fire of diamonds," wrote the art historian Jean Leymarie about the exhibition, "Chanel wanted to translate her dazzling vision of the stars, the constellations, the comets, the night sky, and bring it to the Champs-Elysées." In practice, these creations were displayed on female dummy busts made of translucent, polished wax. Each mannequin was coiffed and made-up in a style typical of the 1930s, imprisoned in a glass cage, and stood strangely lifelike on a black marble doric column. The lighting was dimmed to a penumbra in order to allow the finery to sparkle in fiery brilliance. There were necklaces, brooches, bandeaux, and tiaras. All were distinguished by the elegance of the settings—the mounts and clasps were quite invisible. The jewels consisted of variations on three themes, the bow, the star, and the feather. Each item of jewelry was an innovation in that it could be worn in one of three ways. There was a necklace that could be separated into a brooch and bracelets, a choker that could be worn as a tiara, and a pendant that could be fastened and worn as a clip. It was the first time that a parure had been presented as a convertible set. Whether this was a concession to the obsession with functionality that beset the century or whether it was simple common sense, gemstones had never been subjected to such casual treatment. A set of photographs that the famous photographer, André Kertész, took for *Vogue* is proof of the magical setting which, once the *vernissage* was over, drew an unexpected number of visitors from all over the world. Most of them were in the trade, and they were there to copy the new ideas, the new spirit and the allure of Chanel.

there was much speculation at the time and one might still speculate about the diamond episode and Gabrielle Chanel's motivation in the thirties when she embarked on a risky venture into this exclusive preserve. Of course, this born fighter had always enjoyed a challenge. It would be difficult, however, to ignore the role played in this episode by the man who was at the couturière's side during this period, someone who seems to have had considerable influence over her and for whom she had great respect. All of Chanel's lovers made their contribution to molding her personality, but Paul Iribe—the man in question—seems quite simply to have dominated her. Perhaps it is because he arrived late in her life, but there are two other reasons in this case, ones which were perfectly complementary. Iribe was an ageing *roué* who was used to taking advantage of women and their money without a qualm. Yet as a protean designer, in addition to his numerous other activities, he was a remarkable art director, or what would today be called an "image-maker." The way in which modern fashions have developed are constant proof of the important part played by consultants—the *éminences grises*, the oracles—to the greatest couturiers. This meant that Chanel could discuss her work with Iribe as a fellow professional. He was a talented illustrator; at the beginning of the century, he had produced a collection of drawings of the dresses of Paul Poiret that had made both their reputations. He had contributed to, and even founded, various newspapers and publications, and as a designer he had had the idea for the black ball that is the signature of Jeanne Lanvin's *Arpège* perfume bottle. Paul Iribe had even had a career in Hollywood where he designed sets and costumes, mainly for Cecil B. deMille. He was responsible for the furnishings, fabrics, graphics, layouts, and huge amounts of consultancy work. All of this made him rather suspect in 1930 because he was extremely well-known but had only been moderately successful. When he met Coco, he had just separated from a wealthy American woman whom he had married during an interlude on the West Coast. Neither he nor Coco were in the first flush of youth, but this did not deter them. They even talked of marriage. Was the fine jewelry exhibition a way of giving someone she loved an opportunity to show off his remarkable talent for decoration? Was this why, at the age of fifty-five, Chanel was willing to accept the propositions of the diamond merchants? It is highly probable that Iribe had something to do with it. Coco was not a set decorator. But Iribe was. One might surmise, sotto voce, that they worked on the project together. Who knows what this formidable duo might have achieved had not Paul Iribe, whom Chanel was urging to lose weight, collapsed at her feet on the Côte d'Azur, dying of a heart attack after a tennis match. His demise left the dressmaker lonelier than ever.

as regards the jewelry itself, something should be mentioned about the use of platinum. For many years the precious metal had been used for setting diamonds, but in these jewels it has pride of place. This most valuable of all metals was a mere means to an end for the best craftsmen in the early twentieth century. It was the conquistadors who had originally discovered this strange hard, dense grey substance among the gold-bearing sands of South America. They so disdained it as to call it *"platina,"* which means "inferior silver." It was not until the late eighteenth century that it began to be smelted in Europe and the first timid platinum productions appeared. At the time, the most beautiful diamonds were always mounted in silver that has the inconvenience of oxidising but, worse still, is so soft that silver mounts have to be thick and heavy. They often overshadowed the stones, the pureness of which was often not of prime importance to the ladies who commissioned such jewelry. Sumptuous, massive pieces were more often important to those in power in Europe of the Ancien Régime than their intrinsic quality. The result was jewelry that was sometimes dazzling, always impressive, and elegant from a purely decorative point of view. Those who have inherited such pieces are often disappointed when they try to have an old-fashioned parure re-set, only to find that the jeweler's art was more precious than the gemstones whose value they so greatly overestimated.

It was not until the early twentieth century that the possibilities of platinum, notably its strength and ductility, were fully exploited. The most delicate designs could finally be achieved. It was Cartier that first showed the way. Henceforward, it would be the unalterable whiteness of this almost magical metal that would make it possible to create almost invisible mounts for any diamond. This meant that diamonds could be shown to their best advantage but their transparency or water would now have to be as close to perfect as possible.

This use of "invisible" platinum is a brilliant illustration of one of the paradoxes that runs right through the twentieth century. There was constant preaching about returning to the roots, to traditional values, to greater justice, or at least to greater simplicity, on the pretext of achieving greater equality, particularly social equality. At the same time, a new set of codes was being introduced, a set of values that was all the more subtle since its pretentions to simplification made it next to impossible to maintain by subterfuge. As more and more people were able to call themselves middle class, their lifestyle became ever more cluttered by the useless knicknacks produced by an industrialised society that had not yet been stigmatized as a "consumer" society. At the same time, the truly rich, or those of them who deserved to be called esthetes, were stripping everything down to the bare essentials. The minimalist purge was applied by a society saturated with sensation, temptation, and even guilt. Jean-Michel Frank, the new interior design guru, eradicated any apparent frivolity from his clients' interiors, reducing furnishings to mere prototypes, objects to symbols, luxury to a whisper. Le Corbusier, Herbst, and Charreau advocated utilitarian shapes and created for their few patrons—who were perforce "enlightened" millionaires—stylized, minimalist villas known as "machines for living." "Beauty within everyone's reach," went the cry. Yes, probably, but especially for the few . . .

since the average person still berated anyone attempting to deny him the right to creature comforts. Fifty years later, the debate continues.

as for Chanel, since fashion in dress goes through shorter cycles, and clothing and accessories still represent a smaller investment than architecture or design, she managed to impose on a number of beautiful, wealthy, and fashionable women, and all those who tried to emulate them on smaller budgets, the kind of clothing that hitherto had been worn exclusively by convent girls, widows, and chambermaids. At the same time, at the height of the Depression and only a few years before the outbreak of World War II, she revealed to all the sacrosanct concept of designer jewelry. Hitherto, this was an exclusively reserved domain, with ramifications throughout the world among all those in power, for a few famous firms of court jewelers, all of whom in Paris had long-established showrooms situated in the Place Vendôme.

A brochure signed by Gabrielle herself was distributed at the entrance to her exhibition. It was illustrated with black-and-white photographs taken by the very young Robert Bresson (Chanel continued to call him "le petit Bresson" even when he was well over fifty and had become one of the greatest directors of French cinema). Among the images of the diamond-bedecked wax figures who exuded a strange sensation of morbidity, there were a few lines of explanatory text that appear to borrow from all of the insincerity and self-assurance that Parisian haute couture has always relied upon: "The means I am using are legitimate in the profession I exercise, as long as they are only used in the true sense of fashion. The reason that led me, at first, to design artificial jewelry, is that I found it to be lacking in the arrogance found all too often in an age in which splendor is too easily acquired. This consideration disappears during a period of financial crisis when an instinctive desire for authenticity is reawakened in every domain, relegating amusing costume jewelry to its true value."

At a time when the greatest advances for centuries were being made, jewelry in the Chanel style was as white as her little dresses were black. A surreal, galactic, everlasting white. But even better, the jewelry was flexible, light, and easy to wear. Its simplicity, a complete break with the techniques and designs jewelers had used in the past, is still obvious. "I want women to wear jewels on their fingers like ribbons. My ribbons are flexible and detachable. On grand occasions, the whole composition is worn. On lesser occasions, the main part and the large pieces can be dispensed with. The parure can be disassembled and used to decorate hats or furs. This means that a parure is no longer something immutable. It has been changed by life and subjected to its needs."

Didactic as always, Chanel had found her raison d'être and she set out to produce a personal logic that she could not refrain from turning into a dogma. The purveyor of dictums remains the best public relations office that the world of fashion has ever known. For instance, here she is expounding once again about this unique collection of jewelry: "Jewels are no longer those puzzles, too literary to take form, which the fashion for cubism has tried to launch [what a slap in the face!]. I have found designs that show off the brilliance of diamonds to its best advantage: the star, the cross, a fall of diamonds graded by size, and large sunburst cabochons. That is why I am presenting these sets not in caskets but on wax models. Note that these are not stylized caricatures with which couture, devoted as it is to serving women of flesh and blood, has nothing in common. My wax models of women are as lifelike as possible, like photographs. Some of my necklaces do not close, that is what the shape of the neck dictates; some of my rings can be rolled around the finger. Some of my bracelets follow the curve of the arm. My jewels are never designed in isolation from woman and her dress. It is because clothing is changed that my jewelry is convertible."

What a gift for communication she had, what a model press kit she devised! There is not a marketing expert alive who would not subscribe wholeheartedly to her thesis that is assertive yet concise and resolute. Chanel was also careful in this instance to dissociate herself from considerations of financial gain: "In no way do I wish to compete with jewelers. I do not sell jewelry. I only wanted to revive a very French art, which threatens to become dormant during the present crisis. In any case, all I ask for is to be imitated. That would be the greatest proof of success!"

The grande dame put her theories into practice by handing over all of the money collected from the paid admissions to her exhibitions to charities devoted to encouraging mothers to breast-feed and to "private assistance to the middle classes." A whole plan of action! As she confided to the writer, Paul Flament: "Clearly, the constellations I have sprinkled into hairstyles, the comets that will rest upon shoulders followed by showers of stars, the crescent moons and even suns that I have had made by the best craftsmen in Paris who had been put out of work and were thus free to make them for me—my stars—all that is very romantic. But could there be anything that is more becoming and more eternally modern?"

The future, which sometimes appears to drag its feet, took more than sixty years to ratify Chanel's own judgment of her attempt to reform the world of fine jewelry. In the meantime, there was a world war, the confusion of the Liberation, and the emergence of a new generation of couturiers who thought they owed nothing to a woman who had been virtually forgotten, exiled, and bitter. They thus blotted out the memory of the brilliant presentation of white jewelry with the Chanel imprint. When the dressmaker made a comeback that began in 1954 and even managed to regain her empire (a unique phenomenon in the history of high fashion), Coco appeared to be a greater advocate of costume jewelry than she had ever been before, and artificial jewels were adopted unreservedly by society women as well as all the rest. As befits the century of the common man and woman, from the 1960s Chanel, like Frigidaire, had the dubious privilege of becoming a household name. Little dressmakers, respectable shops in the provinces, Middle America . . . the whole world was copying Chanel in spades. One merely needed a piece of braiding, a fancy button, a dark outfit picked out with gold chains to create a smart suit for the countrywoman "going up to town," making Chanel the hallmark of respectability in the process. The first French women ministers made Chanel suits into their uniform in the days of black Citroëns, Carita wigs, Op Art, and chain-store style.

The diamond once again languished in obscurity, worn only by rich old ladies, Middle Eastern potentates, and at galas in Monaco. High-fashion real jewelry became clichéd. Rampant leftism became an excuse for prudence.

I n the artificial euphoria of the business world of the 1980s across the Atlantic and in the Persian Gulf region, expensive jewelry, unless it was inherited, became the prerequisite of the nouveaux riches. Couture clothing, perfumes, and luxury accessories, all of which Chanel had originally introduced into the market, once again became the success of her company, ten years after her death. This time a range of ready-to-wear clothing was added. In 1984, Coco made her second comeback. By now, the brand name could legitimately claim to be one of the great names in the world of French luxury goods. With an impeccable image and an historic heritage, the name of Chanel had found a definitive place in the legend of the century. The creation was reinvigorated by the arrival of Karl Lagerfeld as director of fashion, and the launch of another great perfume, *Coco*. Henceforth, the exponential success of the little suit and all the Chanel dress codes made it possible to consider cautious diversification.

The directors of the company carefully evaluated, as did all their opposite numbers in the French luxury trade, the opportunities that were available to such a prestigious trademark. Unlike the other large fashion houses, Chanel had never approved of the policy of licensing, which while it might be lucrative in the short term, was proving to be extremely difficult to control and was even threatening to endanger the brand image. Rather than extending their base (a second and third collection, male ready-to-wear fashion, etc.), Chanel decided to expand at the top of the range. Undoubtedly, international observers must have paid considerable attention to an experiment that went in the opposite direction to the general policy of French designer goods. In addition to its daring, this relaunch was in a very French tradition, that of prestige, of craftsmanship, and extremely high quality. These standards were only to be found in some of the greatest Parisian fashion houses. Of course, today, there are links to these houses through multiple foreign branches. The brand names, which are part of the French war-chest, are protected by a French government committee, the Comité Colbert. The committee is a club of excellence and for the last twenty years, Chanel has proved to be one of its most active members.

as an initial, and it turned out, successful experiment, in 1987 Chanel inaugurated a watches department, which was soon selling a range of jeweled watches encrusted with diamonds. Apart from their high quality, they represented one of the rare examples since the 1950s of a line of watches in specifically feminine shapes. Chanel's watches are never mere reduced-size versions of men's watches; they are based on totally original designs. Elegant little boutiques opened like jewel-caskets at strategic sites in all the major capital cities to sell these models, all assembled in the Chanel ateliers in the great Swiss horology center of La Chaux-de-Fonds. The watchmaking fraternity, which is not given to indulgences or passing fads, were impressed. As for women themselves, they were enthusiastic purchasers.

The next decisive step was for one of the greatest names in haute couture to make its official entry into the preserve of the jewelry establishments in the Place Vendôme. Chanel proceeded to do so circumspectly, by recreating in 1993 the sets of real jewelry first designed in 1932 (the firm thus positioned itself from the outset under the supreme patronage of the revered Coco). There were comet necklaces, shooting stars, bandeaux, tiaras, loops, bows, and ribbons of diamonds selected with the greatest care, mounted, articulated, and set by virtuosos. Each piece of fine jewelry recreated all of the emotion, the visual shock and magnetism that the originals had first caused. Time stood still! Once again, Mademoiselle's creations were shown to be as fresh as ever. Yet even though this was supposed to be an identical re-creation, a few variations were inevitable. There was a ring design based on a square shape that combined a faceted amethyst with aquamarine and peridot gems. Its exuberance was reminiscent of the flights of fancy so favored by Gabrielle Chanel, when in the evening she would remove the jewels given to her by the Duke of Westminster or others from their settings to stick them back into a ball of wax furniture polish. Rubies, sapphires, emeralds would be rearranged to suit her insolent imagination. A cabochon amethyst surrounded by cultured pearls set in a ring often worn by Gabrielle Chanel also had an air of faded glory about it. Of course, only the finest pearls were used in this new collection, among them the most beautiful and rarest from the southern seas. There were also necklaces, a camellia ring, and hand-carved agate flowers, each corolla of which rested on leaves of diamonds. There were a few Byzantine touches, including a chain reminiscent of the one which the Grand Duke Dimitri once presented to the young Gabrielle. . . . All of this was fundamentally unreasonable for the first presentation of Chanel Joaillerie. It is interesting to note that once again the economy was plunged into the depth, the luxury trade had diminished noticeably and Paris was particularly pessimistic, and yet it was at this very time that Chanel chose to defy fate and fight the temporary crisis with the eternity of the diamond. And, indeed, all the items were pleasing, attractive, and sold well in the year of 1993. All this was encouraging enough for the firm to take an even more daring step upwards. Right up to the prestigious Place Vendôme. When Coco was still in her youth but boarded at the Ritz, might she not have contemplated on sleepless nights, the magnificent architecture that she overlooked from the Mansart window of her attic suite rented annually through the generosity of her titled retinue? Might not the bronze column in the center of the square, erected by Napoleon, be in some way her center of gravity? *Le Temps Chanel*, her version of Greenwich?

On November 18, 1997, Chanel Joaillerie opened in the Place

Vendôme, right opposite the Ritz. It was a shop but it looked more like a palace. Behind the façade identical to its neighbors and erected by the architect Jules Hardouin-Mansart in the seventeenth century, 18, Place Vendôme hides the former Hôtel de Cressart, an aristocrat's mansion. The vagaries of fortune have changed the functions, proportions, and purpose of the mansion, and Chanel chose it for its collections of precious jewels while restoring it to something of its former splendor. The inevitable Chinese screens, sparkling rock crystals, pale woods, and satiny Louis XVI *bergères* were installed along with oriental rugs laid over beige fitted carpet, and even a portrait by Van Dongen, in other words a few of Gabrielle's personal touches. At 18, Place Vendôme, one is dazzled, but not out of one's depth. And if there is a feeling of it being "like old times," that is at the expense of "a waste of time"—definitely not part of the company's philosophy that is always keen to embrace "today's fresh, vivacious and novel ideas." Behind the reinforced glass show windows, this time around the creations owe little to the past. Yet they are faithful to a history and enshrine a spirit. "Jewels should be viewed with innocence, with naïveté, as one would view an apple tree in blossom from the road as you drive quickly by it in a car." This saying by Gabrielle remains the watchword that motivates with redoubled energy the young creative team that the firm has brought in to continue the jewelry department on a firm footing.

The Chanel boutique is already one of the most important addresses in the Place Vendôme, though it is very different from the rest. Unlike many of those in an industry in which signs of ostentation often appear to predominate over the concept of good design—despite the fact that good taste is the very essence of luxury —Chanel only puts its trademark on jewelry dominated by an originality that separates it from all the other products of French quality jewelry. With its elegance, sobriety, and purity, the very antithesis of chocolate-box prettiness and an overblown look, each ornament is in perfect harmony with contemporary philosophy and there is no fear of it failing to combine with the most recent fashion designs, the new spirit in couture that is once again overturning all previous notions. The grande Mademoiselle herself confirmed this very point by explaining: "Luxury is not the opposite of poverty, it is the opposite of vulgarity."

Chanel is dedicated to taking every liberty in its interpretation of the future on the basis of elements borrowed from the past. Thus, almost a century after its founder took her first steps in the world of fashion that she would eventually come to rule, her dearest wish has been fulfilled: "I want to be part of what is going to happen."

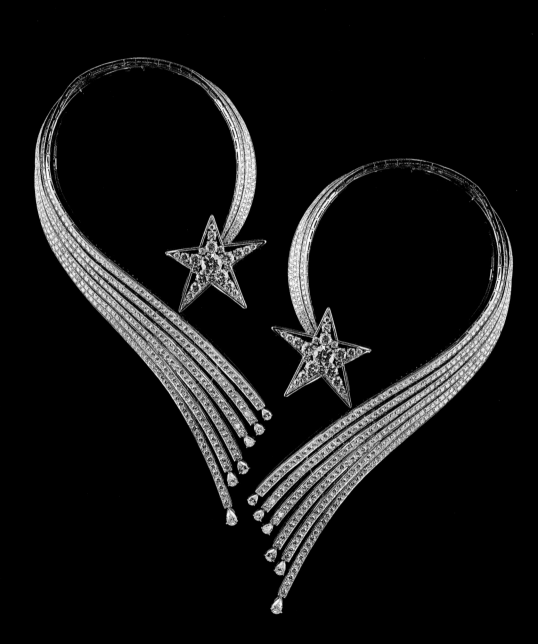

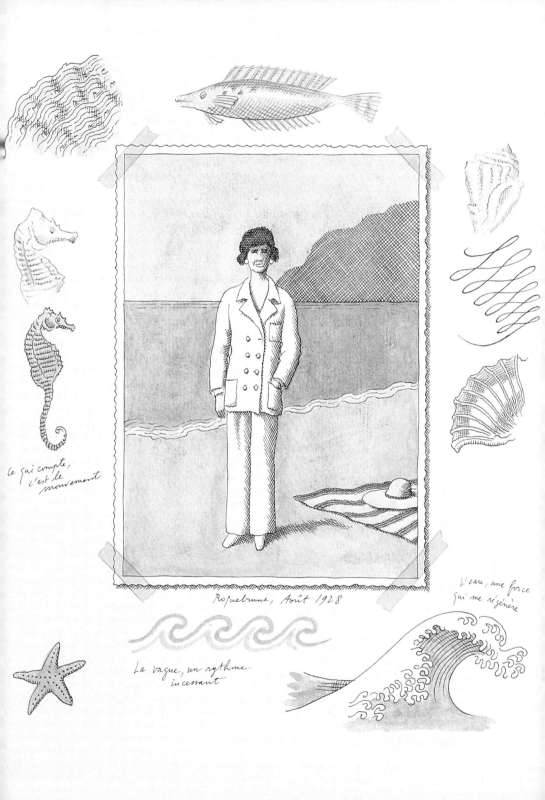

Ce qui compte,
c'est le
mouvement

L'eau, une force
qui me régénère

Roquebrune, Août 1928

La vague, un rythme
incessant

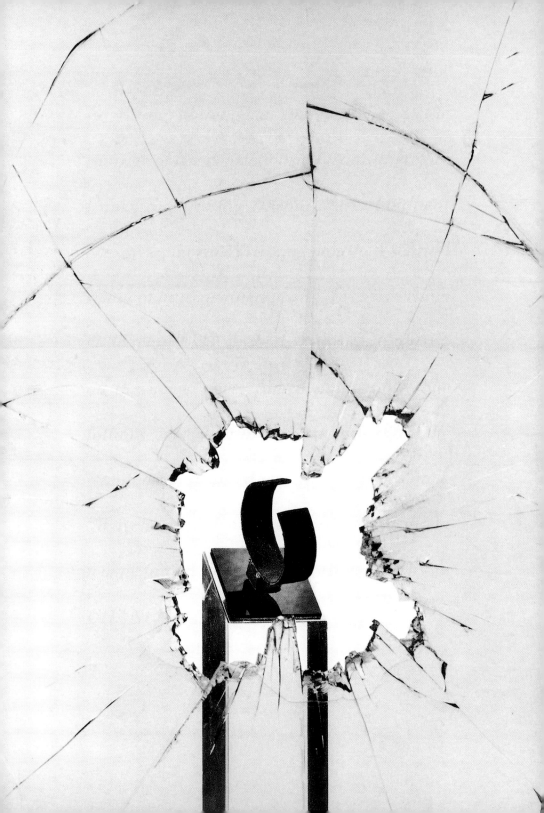

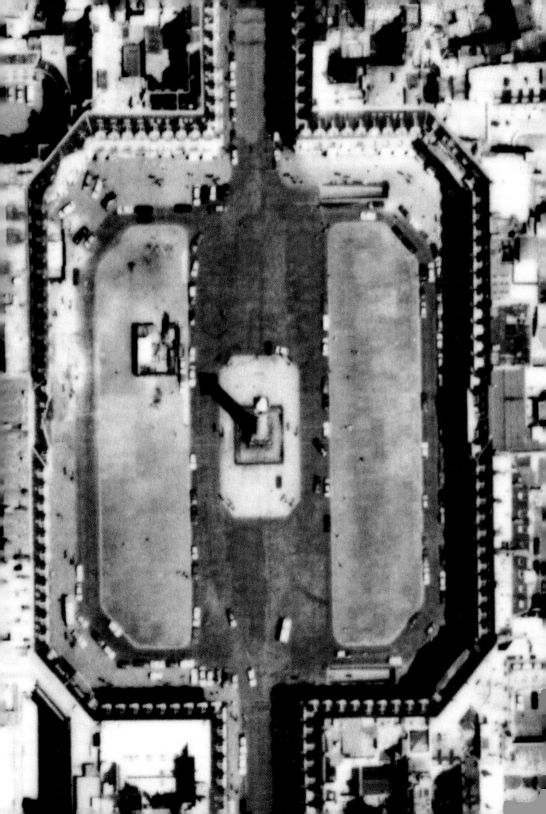

La plage

Je reviens toujours
aux formes
de la nature

La Vénus de Botticelli

Décidéme
la sphe
et la p
tion mê

20 Juillet 1916
Biarritz

D'où me vient cette
passion pour
les perles?

Chronology

1883: Gabrielle Chanel is born at Saumur, Auvergne, France, on 19 August.

1910: Chanel, henceforth known as Coco, opens a shop at 21, rue Cambon, Paris, where she designs hats under the trademark "Chanel Mode."

1924: Creation of the Société des Parfums Chanel.
Étienne de Beaumont is given the key role of adviser to Coco for the purpose of perfecting the Chanel line of jewelry.

1927: For just over six years, Duke Fulco de Verdura collaborates on a regular basis with Mademoiselle in the design of jewelry.

1928: Mademoiselle Chanel takes up residence at rue Cambon, creating a flat whose decor is avant-garde for the period in its minimalist combination of purity and unity of style.

1929: Creation of an accessory boutique within the couture house.

1930: Fulco de Verdura produces a number of variations on the design of the Maltese Cross for Chanel.
In the 1930s, the medieval or "barbaric" themes are expanded and become essential for the image of the company after the interruption of the war years.

1932: Between November 1 and 15, Chanel exhibits her first collection of real jewelry, designed exclusively in platinum and diamonds, and displayed on wax models in her private rooms at 29, Faubourg-Saint-Honoré.
She continues to design fine jewelry during the 1950s and 1960s.

1935: Chanel is at the height of her fame. She employs nearly 4,000 seamstresses and sells almost 28,000 couture models annually throughout the world.

1937: Chanel contributes to the production of *Œdipus Rex* by Jean Cocteau. She takes advantage to affirm the constants and typical ingredients in Chanel jewelry, namely, luxuriance and sophistication as a counterpoint to the severe cut of her clothing and materials.

1939: Outbreak of World War II and closure of the Chanel couture house. Of the five buildings in the rue Cambon, only the shop at no. 31 remains open. Perfumes and accessories continue to sell well in the shop.

1954: Returning to Paris, Chanel reopens her design house in the rue Cambon.

1955: Stanley Neiman Marcus, owner of the Neiman Marcus department store in Dallas, presents Mademoiselle Chanel with the fashion world's Oscar, nominating her "the most influential designer of the twentieth century."

1971: Mademoiselle dies in Paris on January 10.

Mademoiselle Chanel with Boy Capel in July 1916 at Biarritz.
© *Drawing: Pierre Le Tan (1996)*

1978: Launch of the "Chanel boutique" ready-to-wear clothes and accessories for its own exclusive outlets.
Today there are eighty such boutiques throughout the world.

1983: Karl Lagerfeld joins Chanel as artistic advisor for fashion.

1987: *Le Temps Chanel:* launch of the *Première* watch, and opening of the first watch boutique in the avenue Montaigne.

1990: Launch of the *Mademoiselle* watch and opening of the watch boutique, 7, Place Vendôme.

1993: Launch of Chanel Joaillerie.

1994: Launch of the *Matelassée* watch.

1997: Inauguration of the Chanel mansion at 18, Place Vendôme, Paris. The ground floor is reserved for collections of fine jewelry and watches.

1998: Since 1993, twenty Chanel Joaillerie fine jewelry boutiques have been opened in various parts of the world.

Chanel on the balcony of her apartment in the Ritz, 1935.
The building seen in the background now houses Chanel Joaillerie. © Photo: Roger Schall

Chanel Jewelry

The large reception room of the mansion in which Mademoiselle Chanel lived in the 1930s, at 29, Faubourg-Saint-Honoré, in Paris, bordered by the gardens of the Champs-Élysées. © All rights reserved.
Portrait of Gabrielle Chanel in 1940 by the painter and illustrator Cassandre. © Adagp, Paris, 1998.

In November 1932, in the reception rooms at 29, Faubourg-Saint-Honoré, the exhibition of fine jewelry presented at the home of Mademoiselle Chanel on wax models, dimly lit by sophisticated lighting techniques. On the right, a Greek torso of Venus that the couturière retained to the end of her life. © Photo: André Kertész/ Vogue France, January, 1933.

Photographed by the great André Kertész, one of the disconcertingly realistic translucent wax busts on which Mademoiselle Chanel chose to display the parures of platinum and diamond jewelry, created with the help of Paul Iribe. Photo published in Vogue France, January, 1933. © All rights reserved/Bibliothèque Forney/City of Paris. Christian Bérard sketched the couturière as she decorated unattended counters with magnificent gemstones (1932). Chanel Archives. © Adagp, Paris, 1998.

Jacques Lipchitz was commissioned to produce many sculptures for Chanel, including this bronze head of Mademoiselle made in 1922. © All rights reserved/Private collection. After the war, Chanel continued to design real jewelry, such as this cross that the jeweler Robert Goossens created for her. This reconfirmed the reputation for striking pieces of costume jewelry with which Chanel adorned her famous little suits. © Photo: Dominique Genet. Collection Robert Goossens/Thames and Hudson.

The photographer captured Chanel's hand taking a cigarette from a box whose lid is decorated with rubies and blue and white sapphires. The couturière wears an octagonal gold ring, set with amethysts and emeralds. © All rights reserved.
Star, a five-pointed platinum and diamond star brooch dating from 1932 and reproduced identically by Chanel Joaillerie. © Albert Watson/Chanel.

Reception desk designed for the inauguration of Chanel Joaillerie at 18, Place Vendôme, in 1997. The symbols and themes so dear to Chanel are all present: ears of wheat, lions, crystal pendants, and stars. Re-creation of silver engraved with the name of Gabrielle Chanel. © Chanel Archives.
Coco Chanel, with tanned skin and short hair at the table with her friend Serge Lifar, wearing a casual mixture of real and costume jewelry. © Société des Bains de Mer.

Fringes diamond bracelet, created in 1932. © Photo: Robert Bresson/Chanel Archives.
Portrait of Gabrielle Chanel by Éric. © All rights reserved/Special Collection, Bill Blass, New York.

Necklace designed by Chanel in the late 1930s. At the time, Chanel was inspired by Indian jewelry in her own collection. Photo: François Kollar. © Ministry of Culture, France. The famous couturière is easy to spot as she unexpectedly poses for François Kollar in the guise of an accordionist. For the occasion she is wearing her most sumptuous necklace over a simple sweater. Photo: François Kollar. © Ministry of Culture, France.

The Empress Theodora. Detail from a mosaic in the church of San Vitale, Ravenna (547 A.D.). © All rights reserved.
Cross: 18-carat yellow gold, sapphires, peridots, aquamarine. *Coco rings* of 18-carat gold and gemstones. © Photo: Tizano Magni/Éditions Assouline.

Venetian necklace: 18-carat gold ribbon, gemstones and diamonds. *Vogue Gioeillo,* September 1997. © Photo: Giovanni Gastel (left). *The Sunday Telegraph Magazine,* March 1997. © Photo: Kevin Davies (right).

Reverse of gold cross in Byzantine style engraved with the effigy of a saint (1960s). The right side of the cross is ornamented with turquoises and tourmalines. Workshop: Robert Goossens. © Photo: Dominique Genet. Robert Goossens Collection/Thames and Hudson. Photo inspired by a painting by Watteau. Jewelry of Byzantine inspiration: 18-carat gold ring and necklace, cultured pearls and gemstones. © Photo: Christian Moser/Madame Figaro, June 1997.

Carole Bouquet bedecked in colored jewelry. *Coco* bracelet and rings in 18-carat gold and precious stones. Re-creation of the jewels of Mademoiselle Chanel. © Photo: André Rau/Sygma, Paris.
Yellow gold, cultured pearls, diamonds: the raw materials of fine jewelry. © Photo: Laziz Hamani/Éditions Assouline.

This bust was created by the young sculptor **Antonioz** in Mademoiselle Chanel's apartment at 31, rue Cambon, for the launch of the fine jewelry collection in 1993. *Star* Brooch. © Photo: Laziz Hamani/Éditions Assouline. *Milky Way* necklace in 18-carat yellow gold, diamonds, and cultured pearls. Stars and pearls were favorite themes for Mademoiselle Chanel. © Photo: Laziz Hamani/Éditions Assouline.

Two Stars **bracelet** created in 1994, in white gold and diamonds. © Chanel Archives.
Christy Turlington wearing the *Star* **brooch** in platinum and diamonds. *Elle* US, 1994. © Photo: Gilles Bensimon.

"**On a summer evening,** as she raised her eyes to a star-studded sky, Chanel had the revelation of absolute beauty. The eternity of the diamond and the theme of the star, transformed women into queens of the night." Re-creation of the *Comet* necklace (1993), originally created in 1932. It has become the symbol of Chanel Joaillerie. © Chanel Archives. **Céline Dion wearing** *Two Stars*, the *Creoles* and the *Comet*, ring in white gold and diamonds. © Photo: André Rau/Sygma, Paris.

Volute **ear clips and necklace,** white gold, diamonds, and South Sea pearls. Created in 1997 for the opening of the Boutique in the Place Vendôme. © Dixon/Elle/Scoop.
Mademoiselle Chanel on the beach at Roquebrune. Drawing made in 1996 for Chanel Joaillerie. © Pierre Le Tan.

Fine jewelry and haute couture collections, spring-summer, 1998, photographed by Karl Lagerfeld. © Photo: Karl Lagerfeld for Chanel.

Two branches of the same flourishing tree: the golden hands of the seamstresses working at the suit factory, photographed at work, and those of a craftsman jeweler working on a camellia fashioned in onyx, platinum, and diamonds. © Éditions Assouline (left). © Photo: Laziz Hamani/Éditions Assouline (right).

The camellia, symbol of purity and secrecy. Chanel made it her trademark, in its infinite variations, in every texture and form. © Rouxaime/Jacana.
Carole Bouquet wearing the *Camellia* **ring,** created in 1993. 18-carat yellow gold and cacholong. © Photo: Dominique Issermann.

Camellia necklace in platinum, diamond and cultured pearls, and *Camellia* ring in platinum and diamonds. © Photo: Tizano Magni/Éditions Assouline.
Necklace in pearls from Tahiti, white gold and diamond clasp. *Vogue Gioiello*, April, 1997. © Photo: Claudio Alessandri/STM.

Fountain necklace created in 1932, re-created in 1993. Platinum and diamonds. *Vogue*, June–July 1997. © Photo: Matthew Donaldson/Vogue France.
Making the *Fountain* necklace in the workshop. © Photo: Laziz Hamani/Éditions Assouline.

Jewelry and jeans, Chanel in casual style. *Ribbon* bracelet in 18-carat yellow gold and *Ribbon* bracelet in 18-carat yellow gold with diamonds. © Photo: Tizano Magni/Éditions Assouline.

Sun brooch in platinum and diamonds. 1993 re-creation of the 1932 *Sun* brooch. © Photo: Laziz Hamani/Éditions Assouline.
Sun necklace worn as a tiara. Platinum and diamonds. A recent reworking of the brooch created in 1932. *Elle* US, May, 1997. © Photo: Gilles Bensimon.

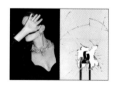

Adrienne necklace and *Cocarde* earrings in 18-carat yellow gold, cultured pearls and diamonds. © Photo: Laziz Hamani/Éditions Assouline.
Temptation. © Photo: Bernard Mattussière/Chanel Archives.

Première watch in 18-carat yellow gold and brilliant-cut diamonds, created in 1987. The design for the watch seems to have been inspired by an aerial view of the Place Vendôme (right). The shape was also used for the stopper of the bottle of *Chanel N° 5* perfume, first introduced in 1921. © Photo: Daniel Jouanneau/Chanel Archives (left). © All rights reserved (right).

The publisher wishes to thank Chanel Joaillerie, and especially Valérie Duport, Mélanie Joire and Hortense Izac, as well as Pierre Buntz and Marika Genty (Chanel), for the help they have given in the production of this book.

Thanks are also due to Carole Bouquet, Céline Dion, Diane Heidkruger, Mélanie Thierry, Christy Turlington, Bill Blass, Robert Goossens, Marie-Andrée Jouve and Jacques Konckier, Claudio Alessandri, Gilles Bensimon, Kevin Davies, Franck Dieleman, Dixon, Matthew Donaldson, Giovanni Gastel, Laziz Hamani, Dominique Issermann, Pierre Le Tan, Tizano Magni, Christian Moser, André Rau, and Albert Watson.

Finally, this book would not have been possible without the helpful contributions of Nicole Chamson (Adagp, Paris), Elite, Hélène (Filomeno), Thierry Freiberg (Sygma), Sandrine Humbert (*Elle* US), Alexandra and Pascale (Dominique Issermann), Edward (JGK), Yvonne Miller, Pierre Pigaglio (AFDPP), Marina Rossi (*Vogue* Italie), Jessica Sares (Albert Watson), Jean-Frédéric Schall, Sylvie Soulier-Biais (*Le Figaro Madame*), Stefano Tartini, Thames and Hudson, and Michèle Zaquin (*Vogue* Paris).